9/3/19
$14.95

FOOD
FOR YOU

Shayna Telesmanic
Illustrated by Kavel Rafferty

Quarto is the authority on a wide range of topics.

Quarto educates, entertains and enriches the lives of our readers—enthusiasts and lovers of hands-on living.

www.quartoknows.com

© 2018 Quarto Publishing plc

First Published in 2018 by QEB Publishing,
an imprint of The Quarto Group.
6 Orchard Road
Suite 100
Lake Forest, CA 92630
T: +1 949 380 7510
F: +1 949 380 7575
www.QuartoKnows.com

A CIP record for this book is available from the Library of Congress.

ISBN: 978-1-68297-337-0
Manufactured in Dongguan, China TL042018
9 8 7 6 5 4 3 2 1

Design: Clare Barber and Susi Martin
Editorial: Emily Pither
Consultant: Amy Reed

FSC
www.fsc.org

MIX
Paper from responsible sources
FSC® C104723

CONTENTS

Your BODY, your FOOD

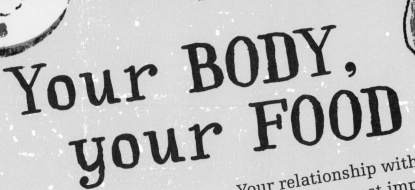

Food plays a major role in your life; in fact, you literally can't live without it! This book is a guide to food, making your own choices, feeling good, and living a healthy lifestyle.

Your relationship with food is one of the most important relationships you'll ever have. No matter where you live, what grade you're in, or what activities you do, food can affect your mood, your body, your performance, and your health.

Get the info, gain confidence, and feel fantastic.

This book is for YOU

Like other relationships, you have to do what's right for you when it comes to food. This book will provide you with lots of ideas, tips, and tricks on how to do just that. Try some out now, others later; customize it to fit your needs and lifestyle. Get into the kitchen, help make dinner, and be curious.

If you eat three meals a day and live to be 80 years old, you'll have eaten almost 90,000 meals in your lifetime!

A NEW FOOD MINDSET

Instead of recommending specific diets or lists of do's and don'ts, this book will help you develop good habits and a new mindset when it comes to food. It's time to experiment with food, explore new flavors, and develop different tastes: the ultimate goal is to have fun and enjoy what you eat.

A day in the life

This book is set up to take you through an entire day—from the moment you wake, to switching the light off before bed. It'll guide you through breakfast, lunch, and dinner and includes plenty of tasty recipes for you to try yourself.

NUTRITION: The basics

Protein and minerals like calcium and iron are very important for you at this stage in your life.

Nutrition plays a big part in helping your body to grow and develop, so it's really important to carefully consider what food you put in your body.

When we say food, what we're really talking about are **nutrients**. Getting the right nutrients from food, in the right proportions, will help you feel happier and healthier. See pages 26-28 for further info.

Why does it matter what you eat?

The food habits you're developing now are likely to stick with you the rest of your life, so it's important to make them good ones.

MAKING SENSE O

How much you eat is a key part of your nutrition, so it's really important to pay attention to and understand serving sizes.

A three-ounce serving of meat or fish is about the size of a deck of cards.

A one-ounce serving of cheese is close to the size of four dice.

One serving of oil is about the same size as your fingertip.

Ready, set, GO!
Nutrients give your body the fuel it needs to get you through each day. Think of it like this; nutrients are to your body like gas is to a car—it's the stuff that makes it go.

SERVING SIZES

A serving of bread is one piece, not the usual two pieces on your sandwich.

one teaspoon (tsp)

YOGURT

a one-cup serving of yogurt is about the same size as your fist.

1/4 cup

1/2 cup

1 cup

The food on your plate

The next step toward good nutrition is to understand the food groups. The five basic food groups are: protein; vegetables; fruits; grains; and dairy.

Why do we have food groups?

The food group system is a guide to help us figure out which foods we should be eating and how much of them we should have.

FRUITS

VEGETABLES

flour

GRAINS

DAIRY

The food plate
This way of classifying food is referred to as the food plate or "MyPlate." For each meal, aim for these proportions as a guide to how much of each food group to include.

PROTEIN

FOOD and your MOOD

Have you ever been so worried that your stomach hurt? Or has an unsettled stomach affected your mood? Generally, the healthier your diet, the healthier your brain will be, and the more balanced your mood will feel.

EMOTIONAL EATING

- Do you eat more when you're feeling stressed?
- Does food make you feel safe?
- Does eating help if you're feeling bored or lonely?

These can be signs of emotional eating, which can become a serious issue over time. If you think you might be using food as a comfort, it might help to tell someone you trust so that they can help.

MOOD SCIENCE

Your gut and your mood are linked because your mood is controlled by a chemical called **serotonin**. If serotonin levels are low, you are more likely to feel sad or anxious, and if levels are high, you are more likely to feel happy, optimistic, and energetic. Take time to reflect and track how different foods make you feel.

Over 90% of serotonin is produced in the gut and only when there is a healthy balance of proteins, fats, and leafy green vegetables in your diet.

Mood-boosting Foods

The food choices you make during the day affect your mood, focus, and mental clarity. It's important to eat foods that have a positive effect, but did you know that some foods contain chemicals that have extra benefits?

LIMIT PROCESSED FOODS

Most **processed foods** contain lots of sugar and **trans fats**. They can be linked to irritability, mood swings, and depression.

Turmeric

CONTAINS: Curcumin
EFFECTS ON MOOD: Can act as an anti-depressant and an anti-inflammatory.

Meat, eggs, and nuts

CONTAIN: Tryptophan
EFFECTS ON MOOD: Regulates emotions, enhances well-being, and maintains constant **blood sugar** levels.

Purple berries

CONTAIN: Antioxidants
EFFECT ON MOOD: Can improve memory function.

Dark chocolate

CONTAINS: Anandamide
EFFECT ON MOOD: Temporarily blocks feelings of pain and depression.

Bananas

CONTAIN: Vitamin B6, Dopamine, and Magnesium
EFFECTS ON MOOD: Can calm your nervous system and enhance energy levels.

Citrus fruits

CONTAIN: Vitamin C
EFFECTS ON MOOD: Can lower stress levels and boost your **immune system**.

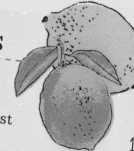

Wake up!

Are you the sort of person who jumps out of bed bright eyed and bushy tailed? Or the type that hits the snooze button and rushes to get ready?

Try a morning routine

A morning routine can help start your day with a sense of power, control, and mindfulness. What works for one person might not work for another, so it's important to form your own routine. Here are a few ideas to get you started:

2 Drink a glass of water once you've woken up to keep yourself hydrated.

1 Before you go to bed, lay out your clothes for the next day so that you can get dressed faster and more easily each morning. This will leave more time for a relaxed, unrushed breakfast.

3 Try five minutes of being quiet and take a couple of deep breaths before you start your day. You could even try a few minutes of meditation or yoga.

4 Set your intention for the day. Take a few minutes to jot down a few ideas, goals, or thoughts.

5 Stretch, or try some quick exercises (such as jumping jacks, or running on the spot) to wake up your body and get yourself ready to take on the day.

6 Take a shower or bath to energize yourself. Feeling clean and fresh will boost your mood and help you to focus on the day ahead.

7 Eat a balanced breakfast to give yourself the fuel you need throughout the morning. Turn to page 18 for some tasty recipes to try.

8 Start your day with a smile!

Don't spoil your day

Put your phone away! Checking social media has been proven to cause more harm to our mood and mental state than almost anything else we could do in the morning.

BREAKFAST TIME!

Breakfast is the first meal of the day, but there's lots of research to suggest that it's also the most important. After a good night's sleep, you've gone 10—12 hours without food, and your body needs nourishment.

The benefits of breakfast

A well-balanced breakfast provides steady and sustained energy during the day, allowing you to feel energized.

A healthy breakfast kick starts your **metabolism**—telling your body to burn **calories** as fuel rather than storing them as fat.

Studies have shown that eating breakfast can lead to better grades, higher IQ, and improved concentration.

Thinking about Skipping Breakfast?

Mornings can be busy, but it's important to make time for breakfast. Why?

★ If you miss breakfast, you miss out on key vitamins and minerals when you need them most. This can leave you tired, cranky, and angry.

★ If you don't eat something in the morning, you will be very hungry by lunch and therefore willing to eat anything you can get your hands on. We don't make the best food choices when we are hungry!

★ Skipping breakfast can make it harder to focus, and easy to forget—not a good combination for someone in school.

★ Skipping breakfast has also been proven to increase the risk of obesity.

THE BUZZ ON COFFEE

We live in a fast-paced world where we rush from one activity to the next and many of us rely on caffeine for an energy boost. The occasional cappuccino won't have a negative long-term effect on your health but, as a teen, a daily cup of joe might not be the best choice.

WHY?

★ Coffee can interfere with sleep patterns
★ Coffee can reduce nutritional intake
★ Coffee can make you feel jittery or scattered

Have a test coming up?

Try reviewing your notes while you eat breakfast. Studies have shown that memory is improved when your brain is properly fueled.

BREAKFAST CHOICES

Start the day making good choices, as a poorly chosen breakfast can limit your attention span, leave your tummy grumbling, and make you crave sugar.

Best breakfast foods
Your first meal of the day should include protein, whole grains, and a fruit or vegetable. For example:

* Greek yogurt with whole grain cereal and a sprinkle of nuts

* a homemade smoothie (see page 18)

* oatmeal with a handful of blueberries

* scrambled eggs on a slice of whole wheat toast

* poached eggs with spinach and tomato

* 1–2 slices of whole wheat toast with avocado or nut butter

What sort of cereal is best?

Try to choose a breakfast cereal that has whole grain listed as the first ingredient and contains less than 10 grams of added sugar. Oatmeal and bran cereal are great choices because they both contain lots of fiber and protein.

Foods to choose less often

There are lots of other breakfast foods available and many are fine as an occasional treat, but might not be the best choices to pick every day. Here's a few to watch out for:

Sugary beverages
Adding fruit to your diet is a good idea, but watch out for fruit juices that are high in sugar.

Sugary cereal
Cereal can be a healthy choice, but sugary varieties are highly processed and contain artificial flavors.

Doughnuts and toaster pastries
These may be quick to grab if you're on the go, but can be very high in sugar and are no better than candy bars or cakes.

HELLO HYDRATION!

Your brain needs water to work properly, so it's important to keep yourself hydrated. Each morning, chop up some fruit and add it to a bottle of water. Take your bottle with you so that you have a tasty infused drink throughout the day.

Experiment with flavor combinations, such as:
★ strawberry and mint
★ lemon and lime
★ blueberry and lemon

Waffles, pancakes, store-bought granola bars, and muffins can be good choices if made with whole grains and contain less than 10 grams of added sugar per serving. Rather than topping pancakes and waffles with REAL maple syrup, why not try fresh fruit or Greek yogurt?

COOK IT UP!
Breakfast

RISE & SHINE SMOOTHIE

INGREDIENTS

1 frozen banana, broken into chunks
1 handful of spinach, washed
½ an apple, cored and chopped
8 oz green grapes
6 oz vanilla Greek yogurt
4 oz milk or water
1 handful of ice

Place all ingredients into a blender and blend until smooth. Pour into glasses and serve.

VARIATIONS TO TRY

Seasonal fruit: strawberry, pineapple, peach
Other liquids: coconut water, almond milk
Supercharges: whey or protein powder, chia seeds, flaxseed

Prep in advance
Wash, clean, and chop fruit and veggies for your recipe on Sunday. Place in a sealable bag and store in the fridge. In the morning, pour the contents of the bag into the blender, add yogurt, and blend!

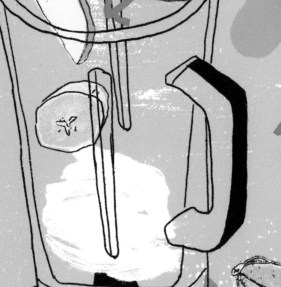

PEANUT BUTTER BURRITO

INGREDIENTS

1 whole wheat tortilla
1 tbsp peanut butter
1 banana, sliced
1 tsp honey
½ tsp cinnamon

1 Heat tortilla in microwave for 15 seconds to soften.

2 Spread on peanut butter and layer banana slices on top.

3 Drizzle with honey, sprinkle on cinnamon, and roll the tortilla to finish.

Go nuts!

Try to use peanut butter that is made from 100% peanuts: it has no added salt, sugar, or palm oil, and is just as tasty!

SOMETHING EGGS-TRA SPECIAL

Did you know that eggs are super-nutritious and are packed with protein? They make a quick and easy breakfast:

HARD BOILED

Place eggs in a saucepan and cover with some cold water. Over a high heat, bring water to a boil. Once water is boiling, cover with a lid. Let the eggs sit for 12 minutes. Drain water and soak in ice water. Tap to crack, and carefully peel the shells.

Store in the fridge for up to one week to have an egg every day for breakfast.

SCRAMBLED

Crack three eggs into a bowl. Beat in a splash of milk. Heat oil in frying pan over medium heat. Pour in the eggs. Once eggs begin to set, use a rubber spatula to pull eggs across the pan, to create large cooked curds. Season with salt and pepper and serve hot.

19

Let's Lunch!

Lunch picks up where breakfast left off—it keeps you going throughout the afternoon. What you eat at lunch can affect your digestion, mood, and performance.

a salad with feta cheese

Foods to eat

Try to include some of these to give your body a boost:

Chickpeas, lentils, beans, lean meat, dark leafy greens, and dried fruits.
All of these contain iron, which is important in teen diets.

Eggs, brazil nuts, almonds, and turkey.
All of these contain zinc which helps prevent acne and boosts the immune system. Zinc, can't be stored in the body, so it's important to top up every day.

WHY is lunch important?

Lunch gives your brain fuel throughout the afternoon.

If you eat a balanced lunch, you're more likely to avoid snacking or overeating at dinner time.

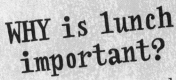

turkey and vegetable kebab

POWER PACKING

Sometimes we may not have much time for a long lunch, but we know our bodies need energy. If you're in a rush, choose foods that provide energy, but are easy to eat, such as cheese sticks, yogurt, rolled slices of lunch meat, pepper strips, or a banana.

a homemade soup and a wholewheat roll

Vegetables and foods rich in healthy fats. These give your body a balance of **glucose**, fats, and other nutrients that are digested slowly and provide sustained energy throughout the afternoon.

Fish, such as tuna, salmon, or mackerel. Fish contains Omega 3 fatty acids which boost your brain.

AVOID THE AFTER-LUNCH SLUMP

Pizza, cookies, and chips may sound tasty, but some carbs can leave you feeling tired and groggy after lunch. Protein, fruits, veg, and whole grains, however, will keep you going throughout the afternoon.

Lunch at School

Lunch at school is a great time to be healthy as well as social. Try to find the time to take a break, eat, and catch up on gossip before your afternoon classes.

Bring it or buy it?

Your parents might still have a big say in what you eat for breakfast and dinner when you're at home, but lunch is your chance to think for yourself and make your own choices. Whether you decide to pack your own lunch or buy from the school cafeteria, here a few benefits and tips:

Packing your own lunch means that you know exactly what's in it.

A packed lunch saves you from worrying about choosing food from the cafeteria or store when you're hungry or in a hurry.

Packed lunches are a great way to save money.

Use reusable plastic containers to minimize your carbon footprint and to keep your food fresh.

Eat the rainbow! Pick a food of each color of the rainbow to prepare and eat at lunch.

SO LONG, SODA!

If you just love soda and can't avoid it completely, think of it as a treat that you reward yourself with, instead of drinking it every day.

WHY IS SODA BAD?

- Soda provides calories but no good nutrients
- It can be addictive
- Drinking soda can lead to serious health issues including cavities, weight gain, and type 2 diabetes

Studies have shown that we mimic the choices our friends make when we eat with them.

CAFETERIA LUNCHES

Take advantage of the variety of food options available— mix it up each day and try new things.

You'll save time before school if you have a cafeteria lunch because you won't need to prepare your lunch.

Having a hot lunch can be nice on a cold day and will fill you up if you're staying for after-school activities.

COOK IT UP!
Lunch

PITA POCKET

INGREDIENTS

1 whole wheat pita
1 tbsp hummus (see recipe on pages 32-33)
a handful of your main filling (e.g. grilled chicken or falafels)
a handful of chopped vegetables

"ZOODLE" MASON JAR SALAD

INGREDIENTS

1 zucchini, spiralized
¼ cup sliced sundried tomato
½ red or yellow bell pepper, chopped
¼ cup kalamata olives, chopped
½ cup feta, cubed
1 tbsp avocado and lime salad dressing

1 In a clean quart mason jar, layer the zucchini noodles at the bottom.

2 Layer on sundried tomatoes, bell peppers, olives, and feta.

3 When it's time for lunch, pour the dressing into the jar. Stir to combine and eat your salad straight out of the jar.

AVOCADO AND LIME SALAD DRESSING

This zingy dressing with go well with a mixed salad.

INGREDIENTS

1 avocado, peeled and stoned
1 tbsp lime juice
1 tbsp garlic, minced
¼ cup fresh cilantro, stems removed
¼ cup Greek yogurt
3 tbsp olive oil
a pinch of salt and pepper

1 Blend all ingredients except water in a blender or food processor.

2 You should be able to easily pour your dressing, so if it feels too thick, add a dash of water.

BENTO BOX

INGREDIENTS

½ sweet potato, peeled
2 tbsp olive oil
8 cherry tomatoes
½ cup kale
½ cup brown rice, cooked

⅓ cup black beans, drained
1 grilled chicken breast, cooked and cubed
a splash of lemon juice or avocado and lime dressing
a pinch of salt and pepper
a sprinkle of herbs

1 Chop potato into ½ inch cubes.

2 Sauté in olive oil until soft, for about 15 minutes. Leave to cool.

3 Slice tomatoes in half and chop kale into small pieces.

4 Spoon your prepared ingredients into the sections of your bento box, or into little heaps if using a lunch box.

5 To season, add salt, pepper, a squeeze of lemon juice or a splash of avocado and lime dressing, and a sprinkle of your choice of herbs.

You can prepare this lunch in advance—your box can be stored in the fridge for a couple of days in an air-tight container.

Eating for Energy

Food gives us energy, but what is it in the food that does this? Fat, protein, and carbohydrates, together known as **macronutrients**, provide energy and it's important to eat a healthy balance of each.

We measure the energy from food in calories.

PROTEIN

There are proteins in our muscles, ligaments, and blood. Our bodies use them to produce hormones, enzymes, and antibodies. Protein can also help you develop muscle strength that is critical for sports.

PROTEIN SOURCES

Meat and fish are great sources of protein, but did you know that many other foods are too?

eggs

milk

yogurt

cheese

soya

nuts

seeds

lentils

beans

pulses

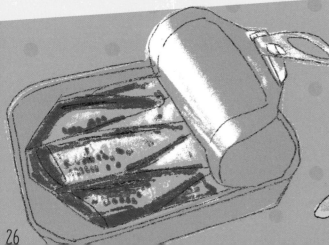

FAT

You may think fats are bad for you, but it's important to understand that you shouldn't avoid them completely. Fats should be part of your diet because they are:

★ vital for your growth and development
★ beneficial for keeping your skin healthy
★ a source of vitamins
★ a great source of energy

TYPES OF FAT

Choosing the right type of fat is important for a healthy heart. In general, try to aim for unsaturated fats and limit saturated fats. Saturated fats increase your blood's **cholesterol** levels and can increase the risk of heart and blood diseases. Unsaturated fats, however, have a positive impact on your cholesterol. Here are some examples:

FATS TO EAT

avocado
salmon
walnuts, almonds, and cashews
olive oil
sesame seeds

FATS TO LIMIT

processed and packaged foods
fatty meats such as streaky bacon, beef, lamb, and pork
baked goods
cheese
butter
cream

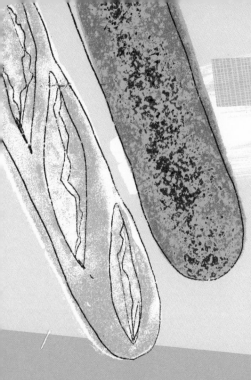

CARBOHYDRATES

Carbohydrates, or "carbs," include foods such as bread, pasta, and rice.

It's easy to eat a lot of them because they're a great source of quick energy and are tasty. The problem with eating too many carbs is that they're broken down into sugar and whatever sugar we don't burn off is stored as fat. Too much sugar also puts the liver and pancreas under strain and is the main cause of diseases such as Type 2 diabetes.

BE SMART WITH CARBS

As a general rule, if a carb has color, texture, and density, then it's usually a good choice. Other carbs, such as white bread, white pasta, and white rice, have been stripped of fiber, protein, and nutrients. These are fine to eat in moderation, but the list below are better carb choices because they contain a variety of nutrients:

whole wheat bread, pasta, and flour
oats
potatoes (baked, not fried)

brown rice
quinoa
bananas
chickpeas, lentils, and beans

Flavor and Seasoning

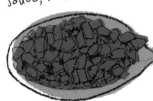

How can you make your food taste great without packing in the fats, sugars, and salts?

Flavor
There are five main taste profiles:

UMAMI (for example, soy sauce, ketchup, miso)

BITTER (for example, coffee, grapefruit)

SWEET (for example, honey, jam, fruit)

SALTY (for example, cheese)

SOUR (for example, citrus fruit, vinegar)

WORLD FLAVORS
Different types of cuisine use their own combinations of spices and seasonings. Why not experiment with seasoning to enhance the flavor of your food? Try adding a few of the following to your meals.

ITALIAN: basil, oregano, marjoram, parsley

MEXICAN: cilantro, cumin, paprika, chipotle

FRENCH: chives, thyme, bay leaf, sage

MIDDLE EASTERN: cumin, cardamom, cloves, caraway, harissa

INDIAN: cilantro, cumin, turmeric, ginger, garam masala, mint, tamarind

ASIAN: cilantro, ginger, garlic, lemongrass, Thai basil

Seasoning
Seasoning affects how food tastes. These are the main types:

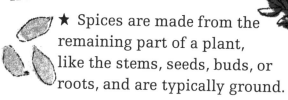

★ Herbs can be used fresh or dried and are made from the leaves of a plant.

★ Spices are made from the remaining part of a plant, like the stems, seeds, buds, or roots, and are typically ground.

★ Salt is an essential mineral that adds flavor to food. It's important to use it in moderation.

★ Pepper comes from a plant and is dried to make peppercorns and ground pepper.

SNACK Attack!

Need a boost after lunch or before after-school activities? Even when we eat three meals each day, it's OK to have a healthy snack to keep you going between them.

sliced carrot and celery sticks

Why do we have the urge to snack?

Hunger pains are your body's response to being weak and under-nourished. Your body triggers you to fight the hunger pains by feeding it some food.

WANT SOMETHING SWEET?

Try eating a piece of fruit before reaching for the chocolate. It may not stop your craving completely, but you'll eat less candy than you would have, and you'll get some nutrients from the fruit.

hard-boiled egg slices (see page 19) with a little salt and pepper

Fresh fruit

sliced cucumber and cherry tomatoes with hummus (see pages 32–33)

sliced apple with peanut or almond butter

Be prepared!

When hunger strikes during a busy day, it's easy to grab whatever is available. However, snacks like some pre-packaged foods are more likely to hurt than help you. Here are some healthy snack ideas to prepare at home. Pack them into plastic containers and carry them with you so that you're ready when hunger strikes!

trail mix (see pages 32–33)

yogurt with a sprinkle of nuts, berries, and granola (see pages 32–33)

homemade protein bites (see pages 32–33)

It's easier to stick to healthy snacks if you get into the habit of eating them.

COOK IT UP!
Snacks

HUMMUS

INGREDIENTS

¼ cup tahini paste
Juice from 1 large lemon
1-2 garlic cloves
1 tsp salt
2 tbsp olive oil, plus more
    for garnish
½ tsp cumin
1 can chickpeas (15 oz),
    drained
2-3 tbsp water
⅛ tsp paprika

1 In a food processor, blend tahini and lemon juice for 1 minute.

2 Add the garlic, salt, olive oil, and cumin and blend for 30 seconds.

3 Add the chickpeas and blend for 1—2 minutes until smooth. If the mixture seems too thick add a little water.

4 Pour into a serving bowl or container, drizzle with olive oil, and sprinkle with paprika to garnish.

Serve this dip with slices of carrots, celery, or pita bread.

You can even spread it onto a sandwich or wrap for extra flavor.

CHOC-CHIP PROTEIN BITES

INGREDIENTS

1 cup old fashioned oats
1 cup nut butter
½ cup dark chocolate chips
½ cup ground flaxseeds
⅓ cup honey
2 tbsp chia seeds (optional)

1 Measure all ingredients into a food processor or blender.

2 Combine until the mixture blends and a large dough-like ball forms.

3 Place the dough on the counter and split into smaller pieces.

4 Roll each between your hands, pressing firmly to roll into a ball.

Store these tasty treats in an airtight container in the fridge for up to a week.

GRANOLA

Making your own granola allows you to control the amount of sugar and customize the flavor. You can play around with different combinations to make it yours.

INGREDIENTS

3 cups whole oats (old fashioned, not instant)
1 cup sliced nuts (e.g. almonds, pecans, walnuts)
½ cup raw seeds (e.g. sunflower, pumpkin, flax)

½ cup dried fruit, chopped (e.g. cranberries, cherries, raisins, goji berries, apricots)
2 tbsp + 2 tsp coconut oil
¼ cup honey
¼ tsp vanilla
a pinch of salt

Whole oats are a great source of protein, fiber, and minerals!

1 Add ingredients to a large mixing bowl. Using your hands, mix everything together until well combined.

2 Spread the mixture onto a lined baking sheet. Aim for a thin and even layer.

3 Place the baking sheet in the oven at 300°F for 10-15 minutes until lightly toasted.

On the go?

You can also use granola to make your own trail mix! In a small baggie, add a spoon of granola, more nuts, dried fruit, or even chocolate chips for a quick and easy on-the-go snack.

EATING Disorders

Eating disorders are common—more than one in ten teens are affected by them. Eating disorders are serious mental illnesses, but the good news is that they are treatable.

What is an eating disorder?
Eating disorders cause unhealthy actions and attitudes toward food which can take over your life and damage your health.

WHAT CAUSES THEM?

Eating disorders can often be complicated. There isn't always a single cause, but they're often triggered by things such as low self-esteem and peer pressure. They aren't contagious like a cold, but friends influence each other, so looking out for one another is important.

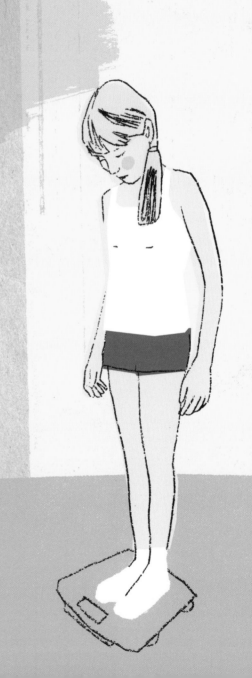

COMMON EATING DISORDERS

★ **Anorexia** involves keeping your weight as low as possible by not eating enough and is sometimes accompanied by over-exercising.

★ **Bulimia** involves cycles of eating then purging. To purge, the food consumed is removed by vomiting or using laxatives.

★ **Binge eating** involves regularly eating large amounts of food and having a loss of control.

How do you know if you or a friend has an eating disorder?

Here are just a few warning signs to look out for:

★ withdrawing from social activities
★ hiding under baggy clothes
★ obsessing about body weight and shape
★ over-exercising
★ obsessing over food
★ skipping meals
★ obsessing over calorie counting

How to help a friend

Having an eating disorder can be very personal and not everyone wants, or thinks that they need, help. It's important to approach the subject with sensitivity and caution. A good starting point might be to explain to your friend that you're there if they want to talk, and from there, seek help together.

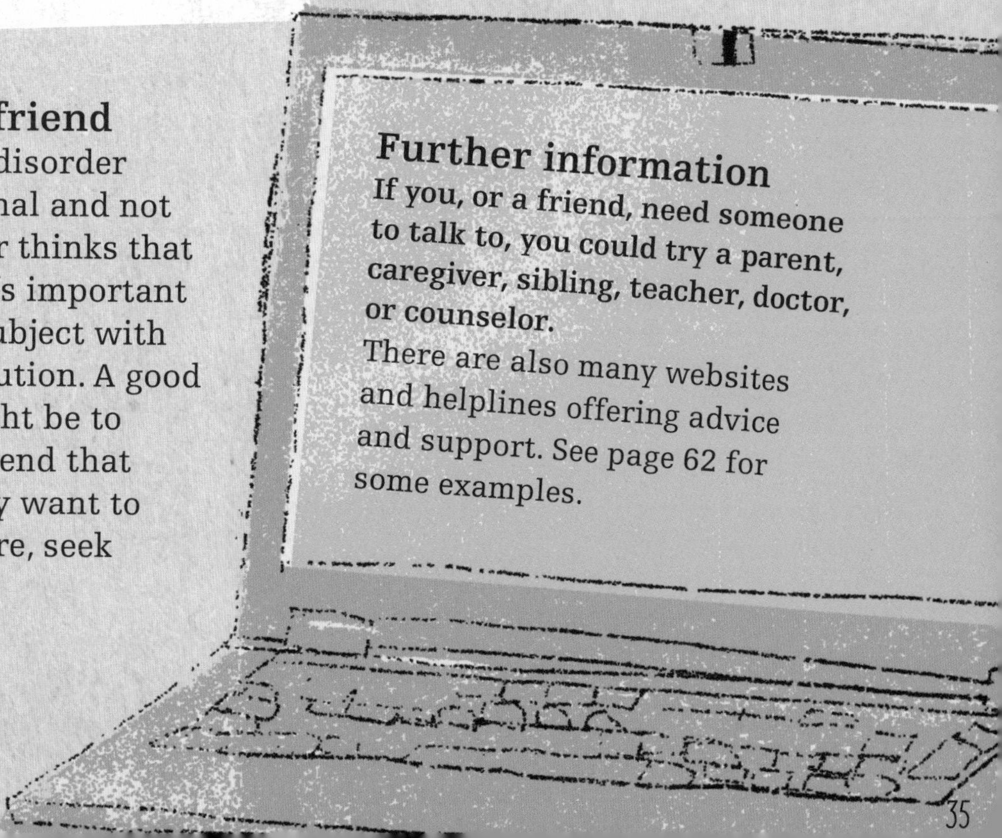

Further information

If you, or a friend, need someone to talk to, you could try a parent, caregiver, sibling, teacher, doctor, or counselor.

There are also many websites and helplines offering advice and support. See page 62 for some examples.

Dinnertime

The evening meal tends to be the biggest meal of the day. While this varies between cultures and customs, sharing food at the end of the day is a nearly universal experience.

FOOD WITH FAMILY

Having dinner at the table with your family can be a great time to connect. Research shows that eating dinner together with your family improves relationships.

TRADITIONS

Here are some food-related traditions from cultures around the world:

JAPAN: The louder and longer you slurp your noodles, the more respect you're paying to the chef!

AFRICA: In some countries, people feed each other by hand to show hospitality, respect, and trust.

PORTUGAL: Asking for salt and pepper in a restaurant is offensive to the chef.

Here are some tips for making the most out of dinnertime:

Participate!
Helping prepare dinner gives you a sense of ownership and power over what you're going to eat—plus it's FUN!

Ditch the technology!
Don't bring cell phones, tablets, or any kind of tech that could distract you from interacting with your family.

Chat!
Ask your family how their days were and what they're up to tomorrow.

FAST FOOD AND EATING OUT

A little fast food from time to time is okay: it's tasty, convenient, and cheap. But there's a reason why most restaurant food tastes so good—it's often loaded with salt, fat, and sugar—way more than you would use at home.

Tasty tips

Here are a few tips for making positive choices from the menu:

★ Be mindful of how food is prepared.

★ For example, a roasted or grilled chicken breast and fried chicken wings are very different. If you have the option, choose grilled chicken.

★ Swap your burger bun for a lettuce wrap or your side of fries for a salad.

★ Ask for sauces and dressings on the side so you can control how much you add to your meal.

★ Watch your portion size and think before ordering sides.

If you crave something sweet, why not share a dessert with someone?

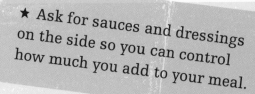

KITCHEN SKILLS

Since we all have to eat, the sooner you learn to cook, the better! Here are some tips and tricks.

Following recipes

Read through the recipe before you start and check that you have all of the ingredients and tools. This way, you'll know what you need to do and you can prepare—for example preheating the oven or boiling water.

KITCHEN SAFETY

★ Always wash your hands before starting a task in the kitchen.

★ Before cooking, make sure you have a clear and clean work surface.

★ Wash your hands after touching raw meat and eggs.

★ Wash all surfaces after coming into contact with raw meat.

★ Use separate cutting boards for meat, and sanitize after use.

★ Store raw meat on the bottom shelf of the fridge.

★ Be careful of boiling water.

★ Always ask an adult before using a kettle, the oven, and sharp tools such as knives.

★ Kitchen knives are very sharp, so be careful when using them.

Pull long hair back.

Always wear oven mitts when removing things from the oven.

USING KNIVES

HOW TO HOLD A KNIFE

Thumb on inside of handle.

First finger on outside of handle.

Three fingers grip handle.

Which knife should I use?

Chef's—a multi-purpose knife for almost any food.

Paring/kitchen—for slicing and dicing small items.

Small serrated—for veggies and fruits.

Bread—for slicing loaves of bread.

BASIC CUTS

If you see any of these words in a recipe this is what you should aim for:

Chop

Mince

Dice

Slice

Julienne

COOK IT UP!
Dinner

MEXICAN FIESTA!

Great for a family meal, or when your friends come over. Let everyone load up tacos or tortillas with these tasty fillings:

JUICY BEEF

INGREDIENTS

1 lb beef (sliced flank steak works well, but you could use minced beef)
½ tsp salt
1 tsp pepper
juice from 1 lime

1 In a shallow bowl, season the beef with salt, pepper, and lime juice.

2 Cover the bowl and place in the refrigerator for at least 30 minutes so that it can soak up the seasoning.

3 In a large skillet over high heat, cook the beef for 2-3 minutes on each side.

SPICY VEG

INGREDIENTS

2 sweet potatoes, peeled and diced into ½ inch cubes
olive oil
½ red onion, sliced
½ tsp chili powder
1 tsp paprika
1 tsp cumin
1 can black beans, drained
1 tbsp garlic, minced

1 Sauté the sweet potato in olive oil over medium heat for 8-10 minutes until softened.

2 Add the sliced onion and cook low and slow to caramelize. This should take about 10-15 minutes.

3 Stir in the chili powder and paprika.

4 Add the black beans and st to combine. Cook for a fev minutes until heated through.

5 Fill tortillas with mixture Garnish with sour cream cheese, and fresh cilantro.

FRESH GUACAMOLE

Whip up your own guacamole by mixing these:

INGREDIENTS

2 ripe avocados, mashed
1 small tomato, diced
½ red onion, diced
juice from lime
cilantro, chopped
a pinch of salt and pepper

SIZZLING SALSA

Mix together these ingredients to make the perfect salsa:

INGREDIENTS

3 tomatoes, diced
½ small red onion, diced
1 clove garlic, minced

juice from 1 lime
cilantro, chopped
a pinch of salt and pepper

PERFECT PIZZA

INGREDIENTS

2 cups all-purpose whole wheat flour
(plus a little extra for sprinkling)
1 tsp salt
1 tsp sugar
3 tbsp olive oil
1 tbsp yeast
¾ cup warm water
your choice of sauces and toppings

1 In a large mixing bowl, combine flour, salt, sugar, and 2 tbsp olive oil.

2 In a liquid measuring cup, add the water to the yeast to activate it.

3 Pour the yeast into a mixing bowl and stir well to combine.

4 On a dry surface, sprinkle a little flour and knead the dough with the palms of your hands for 5 minutes.

5 Place the dough back into the bowl and coat in 1 tbsp of olive oil.

6 Place a warm rag over the bowl and let it rest for 1 hour. The dough should double in size.

7 Use your hands to roll and flatten the dough into a large circle, or smaller circles for personal pizzas.

8 Place the crust on a baking sheet lined with parchment paper.

9 Spread your sauce and add your toppings.

10 Bake in the oven at 450°F for 12-15 minutes.

MARINARA SAUCE

1 tbsp olive oil
1 cup onion, chopped
1 ½ tsp garlic, minced
1 28-ounce can crushed tomatoes
1 tbsp fresh basil, chopped
1 ½ tsp salt
½ tsp black pepper, ground

Heat oil in a pan, add the onion, and cook for 5-10 mins. Add the garlic and cook for 1 min before adding the rest of the ingredients. Cook on a low heat for 10 mins.

SAUCES AND TOPPINGS

★ Sauces: marinara, alfredo, pesto
★ Veggies: mushroom, olives, spinach
★ Meats: pepperoni, ham, prosciutto
★ Cheese: mozzarella, gorgonzola, parmesan

ONE PAN SALMON DINNER

INGREDIENTS

12 small potatoes
a pinch of salt and pepper
parmesan cheese, grated
1 head broccoli, chopped
12 oz salmon filet
olive oil

SALMON SEASONING

2 tbsp honey
2 cloves garlic, minced
1 tbsp each dried parsley,
   thyme, oregano
1¼ tsp chili powder
½ cup chopped fresh
   parsley
juice of 1-2 lemons
1 lemon, sliced

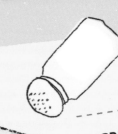

1 In a small bowl, combine the salmon seasoning ingredients (apart from the sliced lemon).

2 Bring a pot of water to boil. Add a sprinkle of salt and boil potatoes for 15 minutes until tender. Drain and set aside.

3 Place potatoes in baking dish and use the back of a fork to smash. Add the broccoli.

4 Drizzle with olive oil, and sprinkle with salt, pepper, and parmesan cheese.

5 Lay the salmon down in the center. Using a spoon, cover it with the salmon seasoning. Add the lemon slices on top.

6 Place the dish in the oven at 450°F for 20 minutes.

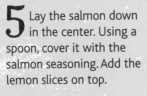

INGREDIENTS

1 lb flank steak, cut into
   2 inch pieces
2 tbsp corn starch
¼ cup soy sauce
4 tbsp olive oil
1 tbsp garlic, minced
1 tbsp ginger paste
1 ⅓ cup rice

VEGGIES

broccoli
red bell pepper, diced
mushrooms
carrots, shredded

STUFFED BELL PEPPERS

For a vegetarian version, replace the beef with soya mince.

INGREDIENTS

6 bell peppers
1 lb ground beef
1 can black beans
1 ½ cups cooked brown rice
1 cup cheese, grated (cheddar, mozzarella, or parmesan)
1 can diced tomatoes
1 zucchini, diced
1 tsp cumin
½ tsp chili powder
a sprinkle of oregano, torn fresh basil, or cilantro
a pinch of salt and pepper

1 Slice the bell peppers' tops off and remove seeds. Place peppers on a baking tray.

2 In a large bowl combine the remaining ingredients.

3 Fill each pepper, packing down the mixture.

4 Cover top of tray with aluminum foil and place in the oven at 350°F for 10 minutes.

5 Remove foil and sprinkle peppers with cheese before baking for another 15 minutes.

6 Serve with a salad and sour cream.

SIMPLE STIR FRY

1 Add the rice to boiling water and cook according to packet's instructions.

2 Add the steak and cornstarch to a sealable bag and shake to combine. Add in soy sauce and brown sugar.

3 Heat 2 tbsp oil in a wok over medium high heat. Add the meat from the bag and cook for a few minutes. Remove meat to a plate and set aside.

4 Add the remaining oil to the pan and stir in your choice of veggies. Cook for 5 minutes.

5 Stir in garlic and ginger and cook for another 2 minutes.

6 Add the steak and toss to combine.

7 Serve hot over a bed of rice.

If you like your food spicy, sprinkle in red chili flakes for added heat!

Grocery GUIDE

Walking into a grocery store can be overwhelming —there are hundreds of options, sale signs, and displays to grab your attention. Billions of dollars are spent to create this scene, and the healthiest foods are not always the easiest to find.

Tips for Your Trip

Be a smart shopper and use these tricks to help you make the best decisions possible:

★ **Make a list** of the things you need and stick to it.

★ **Don't shop hungry!** Studies have shown that you'll buy more than you need and choose unhealthier food.

★ **Shop the center aisles wisely!** Fresh food is often at the edges of the store, leaving the center for processed foods.

BUY ME!

Have you ever wanted a box of cereal just because it had your favorite cartoon character on it? This is one of the many strategies used to encourage us to buy certain brands.

Advertisers also use words such as "organic," "low fat," and "all natural" to tempt us, but often these aren't always the healthiest products.

Food Labels

Food labels are our guide to understanding what we are putting into our bodies. Be label smart and use these tips to help you understand the products you're looking at:

LOOK at the recommended serving size and how many servings the product contains. Nutrition information is often calculated per portion.

READ the ingredients list to find out what the product contains. Usually, the main ingredients come first.

READ the nutrition information. Aim to eat products that include high amounts of fiber, vitamins, calcium, and iron. Products containing high amounts (over 20% of the daily value) of fat, cholesterol, and sodium are foods to eat sparingly.

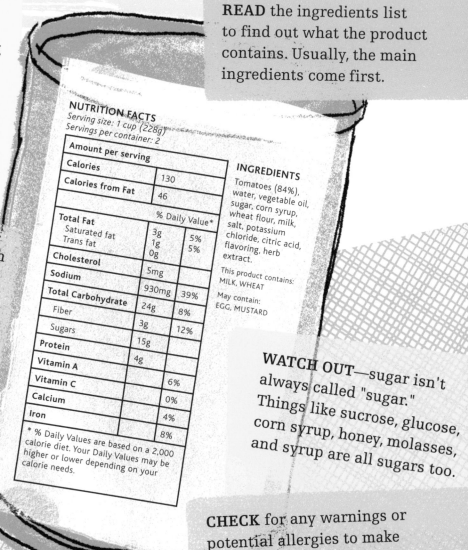

NUTRITION FACTS
Serving size: 1 cup (228g)
Servings per container: 2

Amount per serving		
Calories	130	
Calories from Fat	46	
	% Daily Value*	
Total Fat	3g	5%
Saturated fat	1g	5%
Trans fat	0g	
Cholesterol	5mg	
Sodium	930mg	39%
Total Carbohydrate	24g	8%
Fiber	3g	12%
Sugars	15g	
Protein	4g	
Vitamin A		6%
Vitamin C		0%
Calcium		4%
Iron		8%

* % Daily Values are based on a 2,000 calorie diet. Your Daily Values may be higher or lower depending on your calorie needs.

INGREDIENTS
Tomatoes (84%), water, vegetable oil, sugar, corn syrup, wheat flour, milk, salt, potassium chloride, citric acid, flavoring, herb extract.

This product contains:
MILK, WHEAT

May contain:
EGG, MUSTARD

WATCH OUT—sugar isn't always called "sugar." Things like sucrose, glucose, corn syrup, honey, molasses, and syrup are all sugars too.

CHECK for any warnings or potential allergies to make sure the food is safe for you.

The Sweet Life

Sugar is high in calories and can be unhealthy, but you shouldn't feel that you have to cut it out of your diet. The key for a healthy relationship with sugar is to eat it in moderation and understand that some sweets are better for you than others.

Serious Sugar

Sugar gives you an energy boost, but it can have a negative impact on your health. Eating too much of it can cause acne breakouts, weight gain, high blood pressure, Type 2 diabetes, and Alzheimer's.

Sweets to limit

★ Sugary carbonated drinks

★ Packaged and processed foods like chips, candy, and milk chocolate

If you reduce the amount of processed sugar you eat, you should start to crave it less often.

The average human eats over 50 pounds of sugar every year!

CANDY

Sweets to have occasionally

★ Dark chocolate

★ Homemade baked goods, such as cookies, cupcakes, and cakes—as you can control the amounts of sugar that are added.

How to balance your intake

★ If dessert is served with a meal, and it's something that you would like, take a small portion and eat it with the rest of your meal. Balance out the dessert by possibly eating less bread or a smaller portion of meat during your meal.

★ Try low sugar versions of snacks and desserts—they still taste great but won't give you a sugar overload.

★ Balance sugar with foods that are high in fiber. For example: have a handful of almonds with your piece of chocolate.

COOK IT UP!
Dessert

APPLESAUCE OATMEAL COOKIES

This recipe makes about 50 tasty cookies.

INGREDIENTS

3 cups oatmeal
1 cup whole wheat flour
1 tsp baking soda
¼ tsp nutmeg

1 cup unsweetened applesauce
1 cup sugar
1 tsp vanilla
⅔ cup dark chocolate chips or raisins

1 In a large bowl, combine the oatmeal, flour, baking soda, and nutmeg.

2 Next add the applesauce, sugar, and vanilla.

3 Stir in the chocolate chips or dried fruit.

4 Roll the dough into small balls. Place the balls on the cookie sheet and press down on each cookie so that it's about ¼ inch thick.

5 Bake at 275°F for 22-25 minutes.

DAIRY-FREE CHOCOLATE "ICE CREAM"

INGREDIENTS

3 frozen bananas
3 tbsp cacao powder
3 tbsp chocolate chips
a pinch of salt
½ tsp vanilla

1 Blend all of the ingredients together in a food processor. Scrape down the sides as needed to make sure everything is properly chopped.

2 Spoon the mixture into an airtight container and put it in the freezer before eating.

3 Store in the freezer for a quick and easy dessert!

CHOCOLATE COVERED STRAWBERRIES

INGREDIENTS

2 tbsp shortening
16 oz chocolate chips
1 lb fresh strawberries
8 oz white chocolate
sprinkles or chopped nuts

1 In a microwave-safe bowl, melt the shortening and chocolate, stirring every 30 seconds to be careful not to burn the chocolate. Repeat melting and stirring until the mixture is smooth.

2 Hold each strawberry by the stem and dip into the chocolate mixture.

3 Place dipped strawberries on parchment or wax paper so that the chocolate goes hard.

4 In the microwave, melt white chocolate in a freezer-safe bag. Mix it every 30 seconds to stop the chocolate from burning.

5 Snip a small hole in the corner of the bag. Squeeze the bag and drizzle the white chocolate onto the strawberries.

6 Get creative and add sprinkles or chopped nuts to decorate.

MINI CHEESECAKES

INGREDIENTS

1 package cream cheese
2 tbsp of lemon juice
¼ cup sugar
2 eggs
12 vanilla wafers
1 cup sliced fresh fruit,
    such as strawberries

1 Line a standard size muffin tin with cupcake liners.

2 In a bowl, use a wooden spoon (or a hand mixer) to whip the cream cheese until soft and fluffy.

3 Stir in the lemon juice, sugar, and eggs and beat until well combined.

4 Place a vanilla wafer in each cupcake liner, then spoon in the cream mixture until the liners are ⅔ full.

5 Bake in the preheated oven for 17 minutes.

6 Allow the cheesecakes to cool.

7 After the cheesecakes have cooled, top them with slices of fresh fruit to garnish.

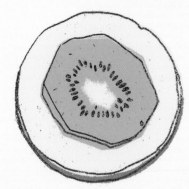

COOK IT UP!
Fun night in

You can plan ahead to make a few treats before your friends come over, or have fun working together in the kitchen as part of the activities for the evening.

SHARING PLATTER

Try this snack platter filled with different colors, textures, and a flavors—it'll have your friends coming back for more. On a large platter or cutting board arrange a variety of fruits, cheeses, nuts, and extras such as olives, pretzels, and pickles. Anything goes!

HOMEMADE POPCORN

Want some popcorn to go with your movie? Instead of opening up a bag of store-bought popcorn, why not make your own? It's much healthier, you can control the amount of sugar or salt included, it's fun to make, and it sounds great when it starts to pop, pop, pop!

To make popcorn, you'll need some plain popcorn kernels from the store, and a brown paper lunch bag.

1 Add popcorn kernels to the brown bag. Add 1 tsp olive oil and some salt. Shake to combine.

2 Fold over the top of the bag a few times. Place it in the microwave for 1.5 to 2 minutes. As soon as the popping slows, remove the bag.

3 Let the popcorn cool for a minute then open the bag. Add flavor toppings such as parmesan cheese, ranch mix, or melted chocolate.

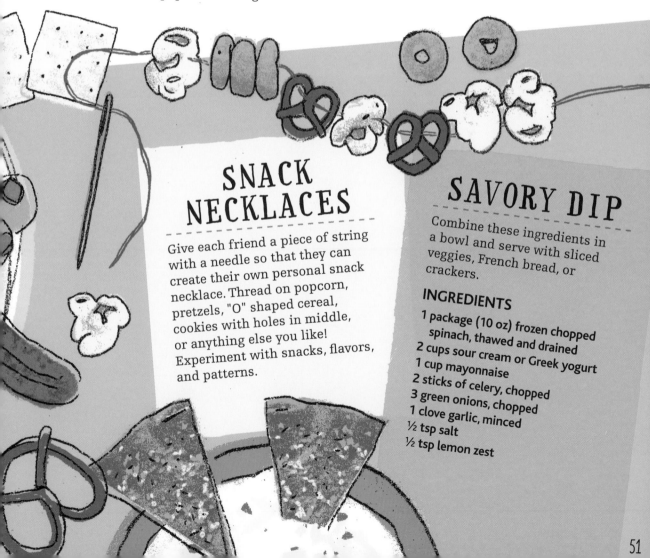

SNACK NECKLACES

Give each friend a piece of string with a needle so that they can create their own personal snack necklace. Thread on popcorn, pretzels, "O" shaped cereal, cookies with holes in middle, or anything else you like! Experiment with snacks, flavors, and patterns.

SAVORY DIP

Combine these ingredients in a bowl and serve with sliced veggies, French bread, or crackers.

INGREDIENTS

1 package (10 oz) frozen chopped spinach, thawed and drained
2 cups sour cream or Greek yogurt
1 cup mayonnaise
2 sticks of celery, chopped
3 green onions, chopped
1 clove garlic, minced
½ tsp salt
½ tsp lemon zest

Homemade Beauty

Who says food is just for eating? You can also use food to create products for your hair, face, and body!

PSSST!

Baking soda can also be used to make these treatments:

★ For pearly white teeth and fresh breath, dip your toothbrush into baking soda and brush like normal.

CLEANSING HAIR MASK

Try this simple mask for a healthier scalp and shinier hair!

INGREDIENTS

3 tbsp coconut oil, liquid form
juice from 1 lemon
2-3 drops tea tree oil

Mix all ingredients together in a small bowl and massage the mask into your scalp for 10 minutes. Let the mask soak in for a minimum of 5-10 minutes before washing it off in the shower.

REFRESHING RINSE

Use this rinse to banish buildup from products and oil. It'll fight through any leftover grease to leave your hair shiny and clean.

INGREDIENTS

¼—½ cup apple cider vinegar
3 tbsp baking soda

While in the shower, soak hair and use the palms of your hands to spread the baking soda throughout the crown of your head. Work it into your scalp and hair. Next, pour the vinegar over your head, making sure to tilt your head up and keep your eyes closed. Rinse with water, followed by a good wash and rinse with your regular shampoo.

★ For an underarm deodorant that lasts all day, mix baking soda with coconut oil and lavender oil.

★ For a quick face and lip exfoliator, mix it with a few drops coconut oil and water.

SKIN SOOTHER

Use this face mask to help moisturize and calm irritated skin.

INGREDIENTS

½ avocado, smashed
½ lemon, juiced
2 tbsp honey

Mix the ingredients together in a small bowl. Use your hands to spread the mask on your face. Relax for 15-20 minutes before washing it off.

BODY SCRUB

INGREDIENTS

3 tbsp olive oil
a few drops of vitamin E
2 tbsp honey
½ cup granulated sugar (use white sugar for a gentle scrub, brown sugar for a medium scrub, or raw sugar for a hard scrub)
a few drops of essential oil, e.g. lavender (optional)

In a small bowl, stir everything together. If it seems too wet, add more sugar. If too dry, add more honey. Use all over your body for a safe and sugary scrub. Store in a container for up to one month.

ACNE FIGHTER!

The egg whites in this face mask will tighten your pores and the honey will help combat oily skin.

INGREDIENTS

1 egg white
1 tbsp raw honey

Mix the egg white and honey together in a small bowl. Brush onto your face and let the mask set for 20 minutes.

Vegetarians and Vegans

What does it mean to be a vegetarian and how is that different from being a vegan?

WHY DO PEOPLE BECOME VEGETARIANS OR VEGANS?

★ They may not agree with the treatment of the animals, for example the hormones and antibiotics given to them.

★ They may be allergic or intolerant to animal products.

★ They may feel that raising livestock puts pressure on the environment and contributes to global warming.

★ They may avoid meat for religious reasons.

★ They may feel their diet would be healthier without meat.

★ They may have been brought up as a vegan or vegetarian.

★ They may not approve of animals being raised to be killed for food.

★ They may not like the taste of meat.

Tofu stir fry

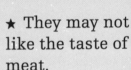

Fried halloumi

What do vegetarians eat?

Most vegetarians eat all foods except the flesh, or meat, of animals.

What do vegans eat?

Vegans don't eat meat either, but they also avoid eggs, milk, cheese, other dairy items, and all animal products, such as honey.

Are they healthy eaters?

Vegetarians and vegans may eat lots of vegetables, but this doesn't mean that they only eat healthy foods. For example, a vegetarian could eat sugary cereal for breakfast, pizza for lunch, and mac and cheese for dinner—all without eating meat.

GET YOUR NUTRIENTS

Because they don't eat meat, vegans and vegetarians need to get nutrients such as protein (see p26), iron, and vitamin B12 from other foods. Good sources of iron include pulses, and dark-green, leafy vegetables. Vitamin B12 is often included in dairy products and soya milk. Vegans also need to make sure they include calcium in their diet because they can't get it from dairy. Tofu, almonds, and tahini are great alternatives.

Eating and Exercise

Nutrition is a key part of looking after your body, but exercise also plays a big role in how well you feel and perform. Even if you eat healthily every day, you still need to exercise for a healthy body.

In general, exercise can be divided into two main categories:

Cardiovascular activities which affect your heart and lungs, such as jogging and swimming.

Strength training activities which affect your skeletal muscles, such as weight lifting and gymnastics.

Benefits of exercise
★ It helps balance hormones which control our mood and brain function
★ It can improve symptoms of depression and anxiety
★ It improves the quality of our sleep
★ It helps to clear skin and detoxify the body

Even going for a 30-minute walk, 5 times a week, can really boost your mind and body.

Fitness FAQs

How do I start?
If you're new to exercise, it's best to start slowly and build up toward longer sessions and a wider variety of activities.

Stay hydrated—replace water lost though sweating by drinking before, during, and after your workout.

How often should I exercise?
It's recommended that we do some sort of exercise 5 days a week.

Do I need fancy equipment?
No! Running, dancing, and playing soccer are all examples of exercise that don't involve lots of fancy or expensive equipment.

If I lift weights, will I get bulky?
No! Regular weightlifting will help strengthen and tone muscles, rather than making you bulky. Adding muscle bulk requires very specific training at high intensity.

Strength training for children should be done slowly, and with guidance.

Food Production

Have you ever stopped to think about where your food comes from? The ways our food is produced affects us on a global scale and can have both positive and negative impacts on the environment.

The food choices you make on a daily basis can influence the global food production system. You have the power to positively change how food is grown and transported around the world.

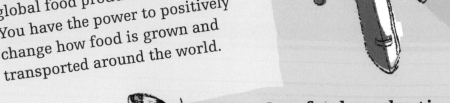

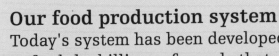

Our food production system

Today's system has been developed to feed the billions of people that live on our planet. We're very lucky that it allows us to choose all kinds of foods and be able to buy them whenever we need, but as a result, there are some consequences, including:

Food and Farming

Modern farming is a way of producing large amounts of food but often requires the use of industrial farming equipment, fertilizers, and pesticides.

Pesticides

Some farmers spray their crops with chemicals to protect them from pests. However, pesticides are chemicals that can have harmful effects on human health, wildlife, and the environment. Many farmers are working toward better practices and are reducing the use of sprays.

Factory farms

Most of our meat, milk, and eggs come from factory farms. They are able to produce a lot of food at a low cost. Unfortunately these practices can take a toll on the health and well-being of the animals and the environment in which they live.

Water usage

Growing crops and raising animals involves lots of water. Today's farmers are developing new and creative ways to grow as much food as possible using the least amount of water.

★ the long distances food travels to reach consumers, often contributing to pollution

★ a lack of awareness of where food comes from and how it's produced on a mass scale

★ harmful and unsustainable farming practices used to raise plants and animals

Being Food Conscious

Being food conscious means that the decisions you make about food are influenced by the effect the food has on the environment as well your body.

Ways to be food conscious

★ **Educate yourself.** The more you know, the more you can share with others and help to spread awareness.

★ **Eat locally** grown food to support local farms and help boost your local economy.

★ **Buy, eat, and enjoy** seasonal fruit and vegetables.

★ **Check food labels** at the store and notice where products have come from. If something has come from halfway around the world, try to buy a locally grown version or an alternative.

★ **Don't waste food!** Roughly one-third of food produced every year is wasted. "Use by" dates relate to food safety, but "best before" dates are about quality, so you can still eat food after this date has passed.

Food for You, for Life

Hopefully after reading this book you'll have learned more about food, picked up some tips and tricks, and discovered recipes for breakfast, lunch, and dinner. At home, school, or in a restaurant, food can make you feel good—so listen to your body, and trust yourself.

Give it a try!

Why not try a new food or flavor every week? If you enjoy a meal at home, why not ask the cook to show you how to make it? Everyone is unique and we all have different tastes, so don't be afraid to experiment with food and try new recipes.

FOOD FOR THE FUTURE

We have the power to change the world by changing the way we think about and grow food. It's all connected and it's up to us.

Food can also open doors to possibilities in your own life. You can travel the world and try exciting new dishes, explore careers in food or nutrition, and enjoy cooking and eating together with your friends and family.

So, what are you waiting for? Grab an apron and start cooking!

Useful Links

Check out these links for further information about food and health, recipe ideas, how-to videos, and inspiration.

Food and health guidance

For further information and guidelines about food and health, check out the U.S. Department of Health and Human Services (HHS), the Food and Drug Administration (FDA), and MyPlate:

★ www.hhs.gov

★ www.fda.gov

★ www.choosemyplate.gov

Recipes and ideas

★ www.allrecipes.com
Recipes, videos, and how-tos based on the food you love and the friends you follow.

★ www.foodnetwork.com
A lifestyle website and magazine about the power and joy of food.

★ https://cooking.nytimes.com
Free recipes, guides, and ideas.

★ www.Huffposttaste.com

★ www.chopchopmag.org
Nutritious, great-tasting, ethnically diverse, and inexpensive recipes, as well as food facts and games.

★ www.chefshayna.com
For blogs, recipes, classes, and workshops.

Eating disorders

★ Eating Disorder Hope
www.eatingdisorderhope.com

★ NEDA
www.nationaleatingdisorders.org

★ Center for Eating Disorders
www.center4ed.org

Glossary

Blood sugar: level of glucose in the blood

Calorie: unit of energy used to measure the energy from food

Cholesterol: type of fat found in the blood. High amounts can lead to heart disease.

Glucose: sugar that is an important energy source and is part of many carbohydrates

Immune system: collection of organs and processes that protect the body against infections

Iron: mineral found in the blood that helps to transport oxygen throughout the body

Macronutrients: set of nutrients, including fat, carbohydrates, and protein, that provides the body with energy

Metabolism: collection of chemical reactions that takes place in the body's cells which converts food into energy

Nutrient: substance that provides the body with nourishment

Omega 3 Fatty Acid: necessary fat important for a healthy heart, brain, and lungs

Processed foods: commercially prepared foods that typically contain artificial sweeteners and/or preservatives

Saturated fat: type of fat found in many animal products. Consuming large amounts can increase the risk of diseases such as diabetes and heart disease.

Serotonin: chemical that sends signals between the body's nerve cells. It controls mood, sleep-wake cycle, and pain perception.

Trans fats: unsaturated fat found in many fried and baked foods

Umami: savory taste that is one of the five basic taste profiles

Zinc: essential mineral that promotes a healthy immune system and helps heal wounds

Index